Alphabet, pen, and ink …

The Letters of our Alphabet and how we write and think!

Susan Govorko

Aa Bb Cc Ðd Eɛɛ Ff

Gg Hh Ii Jj Kk Ll

Mm Nn Ooo

Pp Qq Rɾɾ Ss TtƬ

Uu Vv Ww Xx Yy Zʒ

The Vimala Alphabet™
A cursive writing system
for the 21st Century

The Vimala Alphabet™ and the bulk of material in the following guidebook pages reflects the seminal work of Vimala Rodgers. All concepts for the letters remain the exclusive intellectual property of Vimala Rodgers.

Formerly titled *Animals, pen and ink* — fully updated and revised

Table of Contents

Foreword

As an educator I am always deeply touched to have the rare experience of teaching a student who not only understands the class material but takes it to a deeper level and expands on it with brilliance, immense creativity, and genuine fun! I was honored to have Susan Govorko as such a student. Her book *Animals, Pen, and Ink* is a precious gift to anyone who introduces people of any age to the pure joy of picking up a pen and moving it across the page, forming the letters of our precious Alphabet. Susan is one of a kind---and so is her book. Her "magical touch" adds the qualities of adventure and joy in learning about the letters of the Alphabet. From my heart to yours, Susan---Thank you!

Vimala Rodgers, PhD.
Director of The International Institute of Handwriting Studies
and Architect of the Vimala Alphabet
January, 2019

"The very greatest is the alphabet, for in it lies the deepest wisdom;

yet only he can fathom it, who truly knows how to put it together."

Emanuel Geibel

Preface

The technology of handwriting has evolved over several thousands of years. It all began with an amazing concept called the Alphabet, a set of sound symbols where each letter represents a phoneme, a small unit of sound. Our Roman Alphabet has twenty-six that can produce tens of thousands of words.

Even in our modern times, cursive writing systems have evolved appreciably since the 1700's. Handwriting systems influence people's thinking patterns and help shape the culture of the people who use them. In this book we are learning about writing the letters using the Vimala Alphabet™. The letters are organized by the qualities that mark our own unfolding abilities acquired as we grow and mature and they live in 'families.' We can see how they work and play together in our lives.

Whenever we put pen to paper, we are connecting our hand to thousands of neurons in our brain —pathways of thought that create patterns in our thinking. Since we write the way we think, these patterns form our habits and attitudes over time. What if our thinking habits inclined us to the art of the possible? What if we could live authentically, responding rather than reacting to challenges? What if we had the courage to discover and actually honor our own gifts and talents?

The Vimala Alphabet™ handwriting system is designed to do just that! Graceful flowing letters that support our capacity to experience, enjoy and change our life in meaningful ways. Just as no two fingerprints are exactly alike, handwriting is unique to each writer, and yet each can strengthen that individuality with the capacity for innovative ideas, perseverance, and forward-thinking patterns.

Grateful acknowledgment to Vimala Rodgers without whose vision
and encouragement this book would not have been possible.

4

About Vimala Rodgers

A renowned educator, handwriting specialist, and best-selling author, Vimala Rodgers is an established authority on handwriting—in particular, on the spiritual aspects of the letters of the Alphabet and their effect upon the consciousness of the writer.

Before Vimala could read or write, she was fascinated with written notes and letters, and she collected them in a shoebox so she could look at them often. As she studied the handwriting of people she knew, she began to understand how the letters on the page reflected the writer's thinking patterns. She had uncovered a simple fact: The way we write is a graphic reflection of the way we think; when our handwriting patterns change, so does the way we think.

As she matured, she dove deeply into the meaning of each letter stroke, and after many years of study and research, designed a writing system in which each letter reinforces positive self-esteem: The Vimala Alphabet.™ In this guidebook you will discover Vimala's insights into how the letters live in families, along with the meanings of the letters and how to draw them. Her unique vision includes an animal representing each letter. Animals have certain characteristics that are unique to their species. Vimala teaches us that each letter of the Alphabet is like that too, with a personality or flavor all its own. it's fun to think about the animal whose traits blend with a letter. I've included them in this book. ENJOY!

Vimala Rodgers, PhD is the founder of The International Institute of Handwriting Studies.
She has written several books on handwriting and the Alphabet:

 Change Your Handwriting, Change Your Life. 1993
 Your Handwriting Can Change Your Life. 2000
 Character-building Through Simplified Handwriting. 2005
 Ligatures: Accelerating Your Life Path. 2013

and taught these courses:

 The Psychology of Written Expression
 Sacred Symbols
 The Alphabetical Life

and now offers Alphabetical webinars through her website.

The Vimala Rodgers International Institute of Handwriting Studies
Post Office Box 129, Amador City, CA 95601
www.vimalarodgers.com e-mail: vimala@vimalarodgers.com

Aa Ooo Đd Gg Qq Pp

Yy Uu Ww Vv

Mm Nn Hh

Ll Eεe Ii Jj

Ff Rnrn Ss

TIT Kk Bb

Cc Xx

Zz

The Order of the Letters ....

The Vimala Alphabet begins with the Letter *A* and ends with the Letter *Z*, but all the letters in between come in a different sequence than our traditional *ABC*'s.

The Vimala Letters are grouped by family. Yes! Letters live in families just like people! In the illustration to the left, each line pictures a single family. There are seven different families and a "Grandfather" who stands alone — the Letter *Z*, or Grandfather Zed. In each family, the letters have some similarities. Can you find the similarities in some of the families?

The Family of Communication - *a o d g q p*

The Family of Learning and Evaluating - *y u w v*

The Family of Honoring and Expressing - *m n h*

The Family of Insight - *l ε e i j*

The Family of Creativity - *f n n n s*

The Family of Status - *I X k b*

The Family of Trusting and Inner Authority - *c x*

The Grandfather Letter of Contentment - *z*

Three Handwriting Zones

Writing has a top, a middle, and a bottom.
The baseline is where our letters sit, or run!

hay

Baseline

Upper Zone

Middle Zone

Lower Zone

The baseline is the foundation for the letters. It's where they "sit" or what they "run" on. Some part of every letter touches the baseline. The baseline gives the letters stability. A place to rest. A place to run.

The baseline is the bottom of the middle zone. All letters live in the middle zone, either entirely or partially. The lowercase letters a, o, u, w, v, m, n, e, ε, i (except for the dot), r, r, r, s, c, and x all live entirely in the middle zone. The lowercase letters d, h, l, t, k, and b live in both the middle zone and the upper zone. The lowercase letters g, q, p, y, j, and z live in both the middle zone and the lower zone. The lowercase letter f is the only lowercase letter that lives in all three zones. The uppercase letters A, O, D, G, Q, P, U, W, V, M, N, H, L, E, I, F, R, S, T, K, B, C, and X live in both the upper zone and the middle zone. The uppercase letters Y, J, and Z live in all three zones.

Height and Length
Zonal Balance

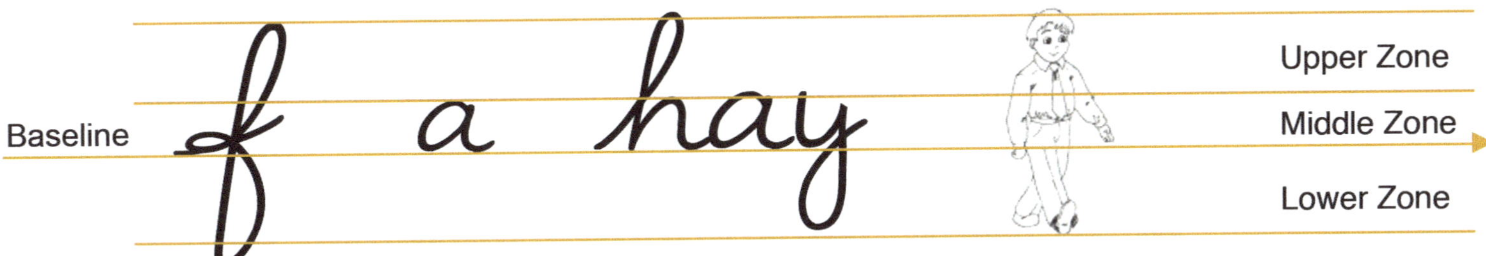

No one zone is more important than another, in fact they all need to be balanced. Just like our body has a head, a mid-section and legs and feet; so too, handwriting balances all three zones to walk gracefully across a page.

All the things that are part of our every day routine live in the middle zone of our handwriting. Things like eating, having our backpack packed, finding what clothes to wear, going to school are all represented by the space between the baseline and the bottom of the upper zone.

Ideas, abstract thoughts and dreams live in the upper zone of handwriting; mathematics and science also.

Activity, how we move and how we feel lives in the lower zone. Running, swimming, playing with our friends. Relationships to our friends and family live here too. Healthy loops allow a good imagination.

The lowercase a fills the middle zone. The upper zone is about twice as tall as the middle zone and the lower zone is about twice as long. The lowercase f is the only lowercase letter that fills all three zones.

Paper Positioning …

Left handed writers need to lay their paper diagonally to align with their left elbow

Right handed writers need to lay their paper diagonally to align with their right elbow

Importance of paper position

A simple alignment of the the paper for lefthand writers eliminates the need for contorted and/or hooked handwriting pen grip. Righthand writers benefit as well, easily avoiding the writer's cramp that comes from choking down on the pencil tip, they are able to adapt a more relaxed pen grip about a half-inch to one inch from the nib.

Importance of pen grip

Traditionally, the pen or pencil is held between the thumb and index finger while it rests on the middle finger. Make sure your grip is comfortable. Keep it loose and easy to move across the page. You can use a pencil cushion for more comfort. Remember, comfort is the most important factor.

The Family of Communication

- Ovals represent the self ....
- Loops in the lower zone represent the self in relationship ...
- Stem in the upper zone represents thought about and perception of self as others see us

a   *oo*   *d*   *8*   *q*   *p*

an oval with a tail .... our natural self.

a clear oval ... no tail ... our mouth expressing; talking.

an oval with a periscope that goes up like antennae picking up other's thoughts and actions toward self.

Sensitivity.

a half oval, like the letter c, open to what comes next, with a loop in the lower zone, our self in action, and relationship with others.

an oval with a forward loop in the lower zone ... self in service to others.

Not a full oval ... *p* is the step child of this family .... a stem in the lower zone ... relationship of self to self; an arc in the middle zone ... self moving forward.

Aa

Uppercase

Upper zone

Baseline — Middle zone

Lower zone

Begin at the baseline with a curved line. This is called a garland.

When a garland begins a letter, it is called the "Lincoln foot".

Make your line curve up to the top of the upper zone.

This is called an "ascender" or an "upstroke"

Next, change direction, and draw a straight vertical line down to the baseline.

This is called an "I am stroke"

Now, change direction again by curving back to the left. Cross over the first "upstroke" line you made.

Finally, form a little loop behind the upstroke, and finish off to the right, beyond your "I am" stroke.

This little loop is called a "persistence tie"

Lowercase

Upper zone

Baseline — Middle zone

Lower zone

Begin at the top of the middle zone with a curve to the left and down to the baseline.

Round your curve back up to the top of the middle zone forming a closed oval.

Next, change direction, and come back down to the baseline ...

finishing with a "garland" to the right.

A "garland" is a soft cup-like stroke, often placed at the end of letters. It's like a friendly little hand reaching out.

The Vimala Alphabet™

Ooo

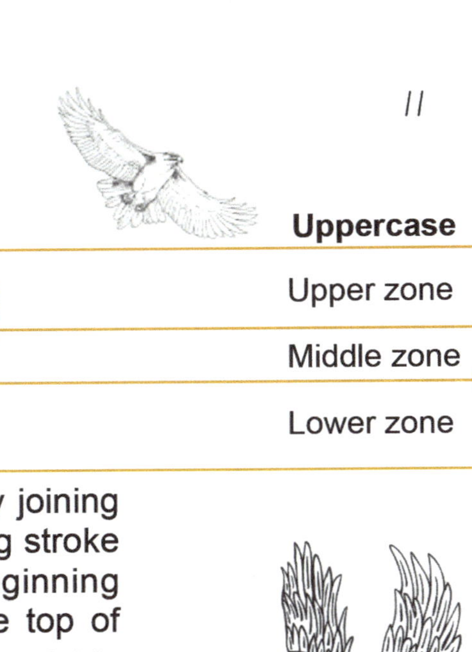

Uppercase

Upper zone

Middle zone

Baseline

Lower zone

Begin at the top of the upper zone with a curve to the right rounding down to the baseline.

Round your curve back up to the top of the upper zone.

Complete by joining your finishing stroke to your beginning stroke at the top of the upper zone. Make it clean, seamless with no ragged edges.

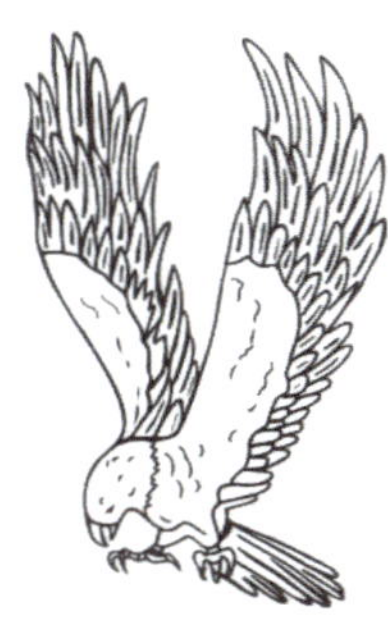

Stand alone   or   with a "bridge stroke"

Lowercase

Upper zone

Baseline

Middle zone

Lower zone

Begin at the top of the middle zone with a curve to the right rounding down to the baseline.

Complete by rounding your curve back up to the top of the middle zone forming a closed circle.

Begin at the top of the middle zone with a curve to the left and down to the baseline.

Round your curve back up to the top of the middle zone forming a closed circle.

Finish with a small horizontal line off to the right at the top of the middle zone.

This little line is called a "bridge stroke" because it links the o to the next letter in a word.

The Vimala Alphabet™

Ðd

Uppercase

Upper zone

Baseline — Middle zone

Lower zone

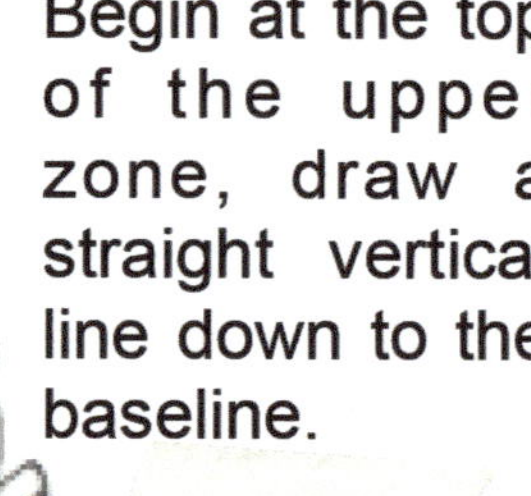

Begin at the top of the upper zone, draw a straight vertical line down to the baseline.

This is called an "I am stroke"

Lift your pen or pencil off the paper.

Begin another horizontal line at the top of the upper zone.

Make it round down to the baseline so it forms a half circle when it touches your "I am stroke."

Complete by turning and curving to the right as you loop through your half circle and finish to the right of your "I am stroke."

Lowercase

Upper zone

Baseline — Middle zone

Lower zone

Begin at the top of the middle zone with a curve to the left and down to the baseline.

Round your curve back up to the top of the middle zone forming a closed oval, and keep going straight up to the top of the upper zone.

This "upstroke" is called an "ascender"

Next, change direction, and retrace your "upstroke" down to the baseline.

This retraced upstroke is called a "stem."

Finish with a "garland" to the right.

A "garland" is a soft cup-like stroke, often placed at the end of letters. It's like a friendly little hand reaching out.

The Vimala Alphabet™

Uppercase

Upper zone

Baseline — Middle zone

Lower zone

Begin at the top of the upper zone with a curve to the left and down to the baseline forming a large half circle, like the uppercase letter C.

Lift your pen or pencil off the paper.

Begin another horizontal line at the top of the middle zone. Make it softly curve down ....

turning to finish at the baseline. (It looks a little like a soft numeral 7)

This is the only letter that is formed with two lines that do NOT touch each other.

Lowercase

Upper zone

Baseline — Middle zone

Lower zone

Begin at the top of the middle zone with a curve to the left and down to the baseline .

Move from the baseline diagonally downward into the lower zone, forming an elongated S shape.

Next, change direction by rounding back up to the baseline forming a loop in the lower zone.

Cross over your first descending stroke and finish to the right. Leave the half oval in the middle zone open.

The Vimala Alphabet™

Qq

Uppercase

Upper zone

Baseline Middle zone

Lower zone

Begin at the top of the upper zone with a curve to the right and down to the baseline.

Round your curve back up to the top of the upper zone forming a generous circle.

Join your finishing stroke to your beginning stroke at the top of the upper zone.

Make it clean, (seamless) with no ragged edges.

Complete by giving your Q a tail ... make it soft and curvy with a little "garland" finish.

Play with this little tail, it's a "fluorish" that gives the Q a little bit of fun! Make it soft with a "garland" flourish. It's like a friendly little hand reaching out.

Lowercase

Upper zone

Baseline Middle zone

Lower zone

Begin at the top of the middle zone with a curve to the left and down to the baseline.

Round your curve back up to the top of the middle zone forming a closed oval.

Next, change direction, and come straight down into the lower zone ...

The is called a "decender" or a "downstroke"

Change direction again with a soft rightward curve and draw up to form a lower "loop" that finishes at the baseline ...

Finally, form a little loop behind the "downstroke," and finish off to the right, beyond that same "downstroke," completing with a forward stroke.

This little loop is called a "persistence tie"

The Vimala Alphabet™

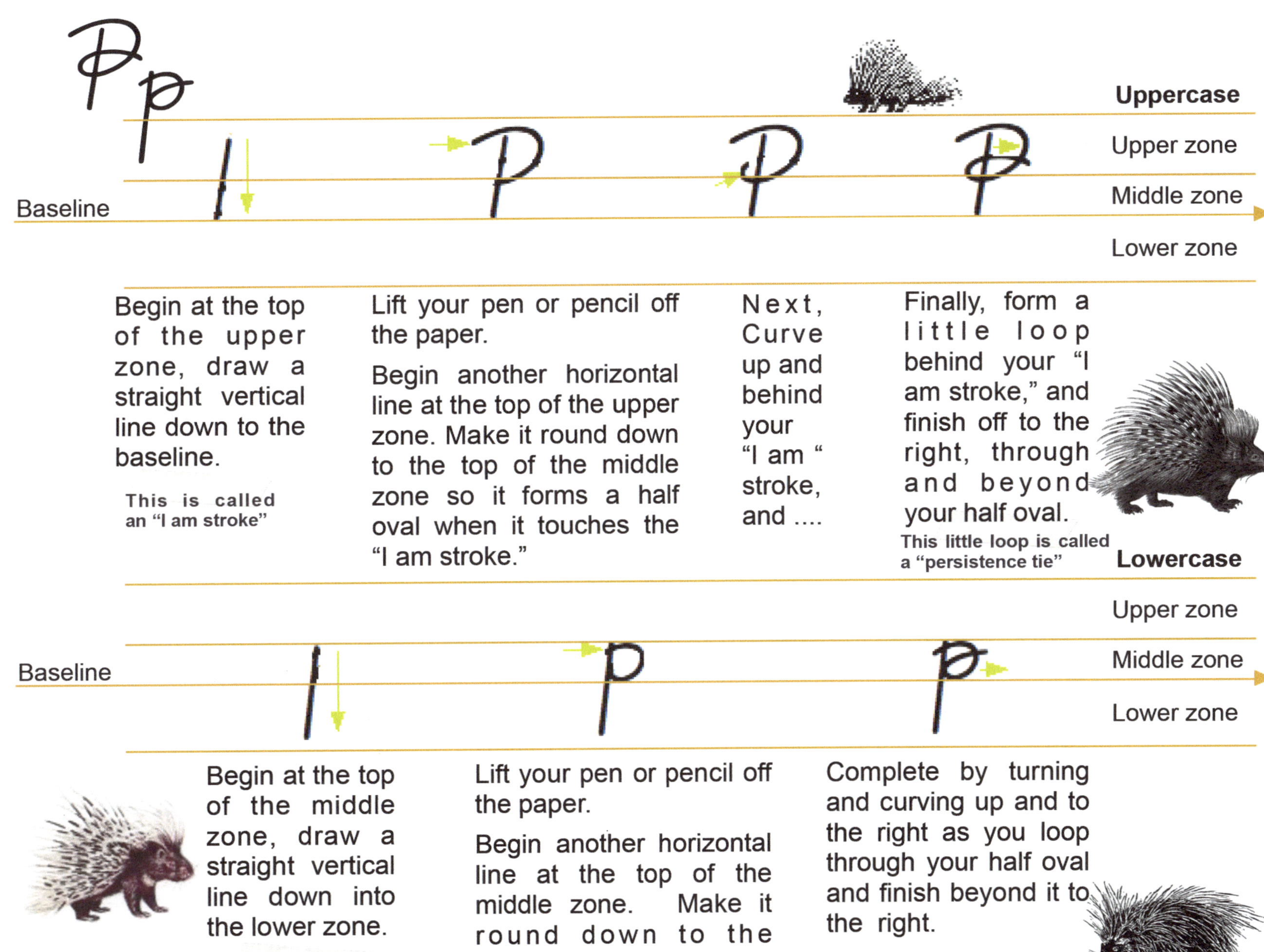

Uppercase

Upper zone

Baseline — Middle zone

Lower zone

Begin at the top of the upper zone, draw a straight vertical line down to the baseline.

This is called an "I am stroke"

Lift your pen or pencil off the paper.

Begin another horizontal line at the top of the upper zone. Make it round down to the top of the middle zone so it forms a half oval when it touches the "I am stroke."

Next, Curve up and behind your "I am " stroke, and ....

Finally, form a little loop behind your "I am stroke," and finish off to the right, through and beyond your half oval.

This little loop is called a "persistence tie"

Lowercase

Upper zone

Baseline — Middle zone

Lower zone

Begin at the top of the middle zone, draw a straight vertical line down into the lower zone.

This "downstroke" is also called a "descender"

Lift your pen or pencil off the paper.

Begin another horizontal line at the top of the middle zone. Make it round down to the baseline so it forms a half oval when it touches your first "downstroke."

Complete by turning and curving up and to the right as you loop through your half oval and finish beyond it to the right.

The Vimala Alphabet™

The Family of Learning and Evaluating

- Garlands and an angle
- Cups and funnels of information, experience, and knowledge
- A loop in the lower zone represents putting our talents and knowledge to work

y	u	w	v
a cup with a tail ... the ability to apply one's knowledge into action; skills, talents, mastery.	a cup ... finishing in a gentle garland, our openness to receive; holds our knowledge and our love of learning.	"Double u" Containers, or cups, for our learning and sharing; one cup to learn, one to teach what we know to others; mentoring.	a funnel that narrows down to channel only the most essential ingredients; a sieve for sifting information, reducing it to the most fundamental; evaluating; discerning.

Uppercase

Upper zone

Baseline — Middle zone

Lower zone

Begin at the top of the upper zone, draw a vertical line down and curve into a garland at the baseline.

Complete the full garland at the baseline, then curve back up to the top of the upper zone. Make this upstroke a little shorter than the beginning downstroke.

From the top of the upper zone, draw a vertical line into the lower zone.

Curve leftward and loop up.

Complete the loop at the baseline, finishing to the right of the downstroke.

Lowercase

Upper zone

Baseline — Middle zone

Lower zone

Begin at the top of the middle zone, draw a vertical line down and curve into a garland at the baseline.

Complete the full garland at the baseline, then curve back up to the top of the middle zone. Make this upstroke a little shorter than the beginning downstroke.

From the top of the middle zone, draw a vertical line into the lower zone.

Curve leftward and loop up.

Complete the loop at the baseline, finishing to the right of the downstroke.

The Vimala Alphabet™

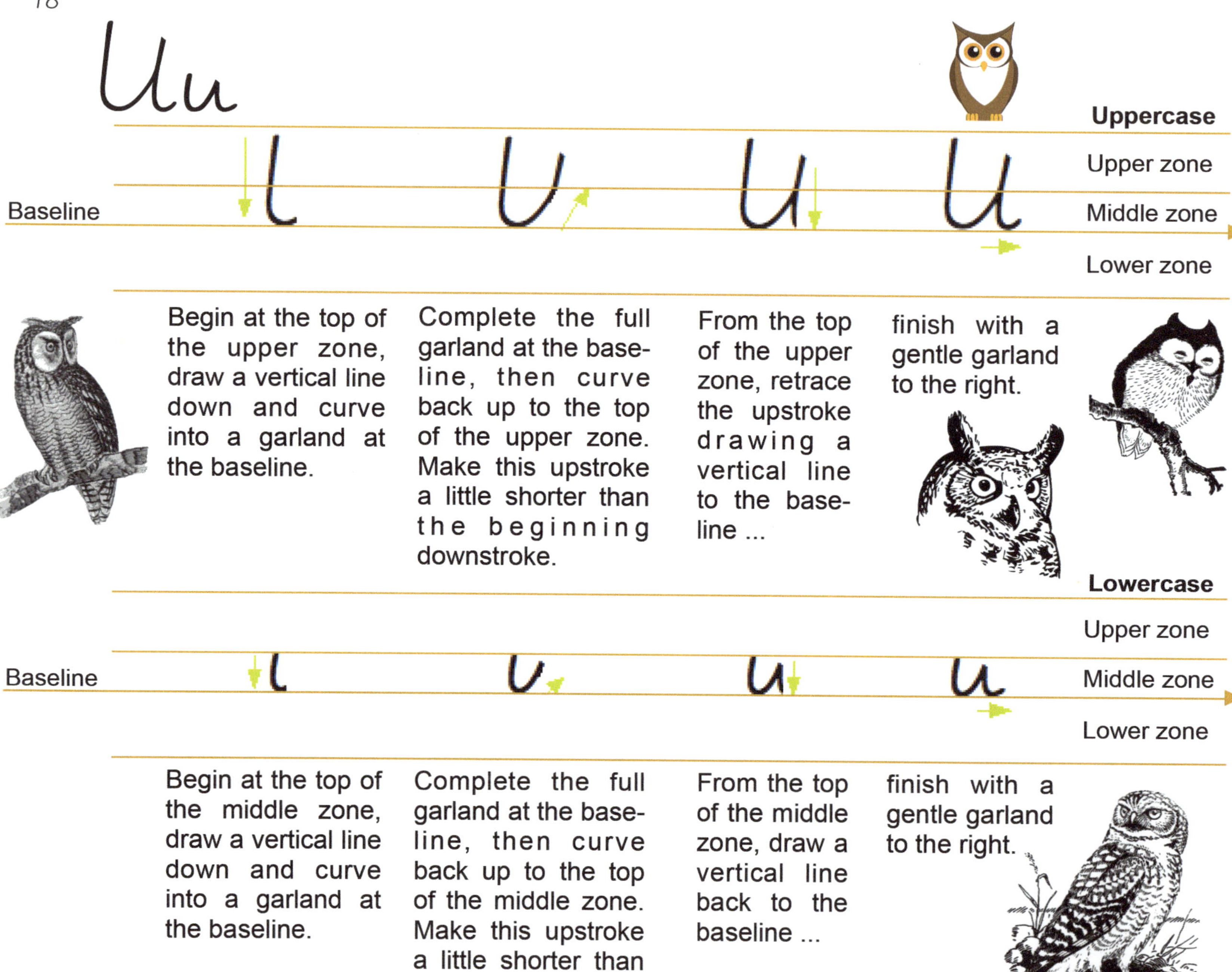

Uppercase

Upper zone

Baseline | Middle zone

Lower zone

Begin at the top of the upper zone, draw a vertical line down and curve into a garland at the baseline.

Complete the full garland at the baseline, then curve back up to the top of the upper zone. Make this upstroke a little shorter than the beginning downstroke.

From the top of the upper zone, retrace the upstroke drawing a vertical line to the baseline ...

finish with a gentle garland to the right.

Lowercase

Upper zone

Baseline | Middle zone

Lower zone

Begin at the top of the middle zone, draw a vertical line down and curve into a garland at the baseline.

Complete the full garland at the baseline, then curve back up to the top of the middle zone. Make this upstroke a little shorter than the beginning downstroke.

From the top of the middle zone, draw a vertical line back to the baseline ...

finish with a gentle garland to the right.

The Vimala Alphabet™

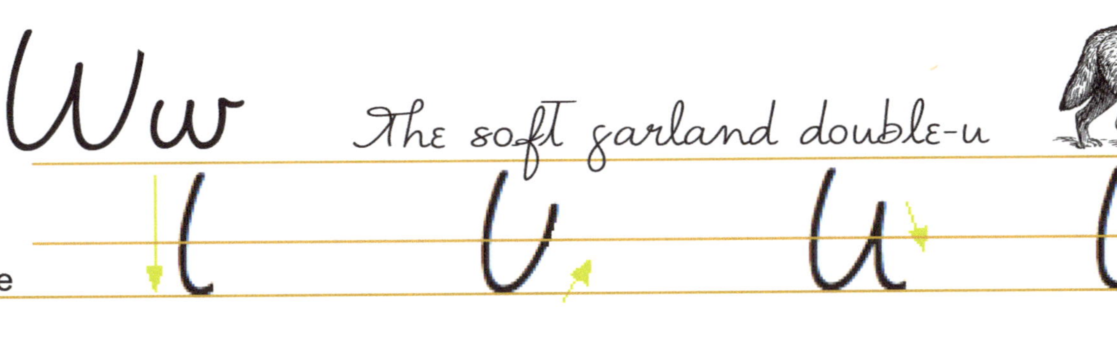
Ww

The soft garland double-u

Uppercase

Upper zone

Baseline — Middle zone

Lower zone

From the top of the upper zone, draw a slightly bowed vertical line to the baseline, moving the pen to curve softly to the right into a garland.

Complete the full garland, and draw an upstroke back to the upper zone. Make this upstroke a little shorter than the beginning downstroke.

From the upper zone, softly curve back down to the baseline, making another gentle garland to the right.

Complete the second full garland, and draw an upstroke back to the upper zone, finishing with the upstroke slightly shorter than the beginning stroke.

Lowercase

Upper zone

Baseline — Middle zone

Lower zone

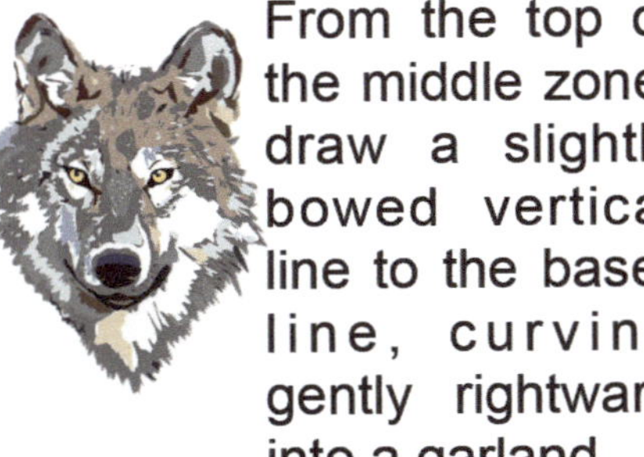

From the top of the middle zone, draw a slightly bowed vertical line to the baseline, curving gently rightward into a garland.

Complete the full garland, and curve back up to the top of the middle zone.

From the top of the middle zone, retrace the upstroke, curving into the baseline, with a second gentle garland to the right.

Complete the full garland, curving back to the top of the middle zone, and finish with a little horizontal line to the right.

This is called a "bridge stoke"

The Vimala Alphabet™

Vv

Uppercase

Upper zone

Baseline

Middle zone

Lower zone

Beginning at the top of the upper zone, draw a slightly diagonal line rightward to the baseline.

Finish by drawing another diagonal line that curves slightly rightward (like a bow) as it reaches to the top of the upper zone.

Lowercase

Upper zone

Baseline

Middle zone

Lower zone

Beginning at the top of the middle zone, draw a slightly diagonal line rightward to the baseline.

Finish by drawing another diagonal line that curves slightly rightward (like a bow) as it reaches to the top of the middle zone.

The Vimala Alphabet™

The Family of Honoring and Expressing

- Arcades, arches that march on and on across a page
- A loop in the upper zone that brings our ideas into play

m

three arches that flow downwards ... cascading like a gentle waterfall ... Divine Grace.

Each arcade, in succession, also represents our relationship to self, to another, to the group or community.

n

two arches that flow downwards ... relating to another person; the letter of friendship.

h

one arch ... preceded by a loop to the upper zone (the letter *l*) ... it reaches to our highest thoughts, ideals, spirit ... then brings them forward with the little camel hump moving in the middle zone.

Uppercase

Baseline — Upper zone — Middle zone — Lower zone

Draw a soft garland-like horizontal line at the top of the upper zone.

When a soft stroke begins a letter at the top of the upper zone it is called a "humor flourish"

Next, make a straight vertical line down to the baseline. The "I am."

Pull to the right and away from the down-stroke.

This angle-V formation is called a "pull apart" stroke

Rounding at the top of the upper zone, draw back down to the baseline.

This soft arch-like formation is called an "arcade"

Pull away from this second downstroke, and make a second arcade.

Finish with a gentle garland to the right.

Lowercase

Baseline — Upper zone — Middle zone — Lower zone

Begin at the baseline with a soft diagonal line to the top of the middle zone.

Rounding at the top of the middle zone, draw back down to the base-line.

This soft arch-like formation is called an "arcade"

Pull to the right and away from the down-stroke.

This angle-V formation is called a "pull apart" stroke

Round again at the top of the middle zone, making a second arcade.

Again, pull to the right and away from the downstroke, then round at the top of the middle zone, making a third arcade.

Finish with a gentle garland to the right.

The Vimala Alphabet™

Uppercase

Upper zone

Middle zone

Baseline

Lower zone

Draw a soft garland-like horizontal line at the top of the upper zone.

When a soft stroke begins a letter at the top of the upper zone it is called a "humor flourish"

Next, make a straight vertical line down to the baseline. The "I am."

Pull to the right and away from the down-stroke.

This angle-V formation is called a "pull apart" stroke

Rounding at the top of the upper zone, draw back down to the baseline.

This soft arch-like formation is called an "arcade"

Finish with a gentle garland to the right.

Lowercase

Upper zone

Middle zone

Baseline

Lower zone

Begin at the baseline with a soft diagonal line to the top of the middle zone.

Rounding at the top of the middle zone, draw back down to the base-line.

This soft arch-like formation is called an "arcade"

Pull to the right and away from the down-stroke.

This angle-V formation is called a "pull apart" stroke

Round again at the top of the middle zone, making a second arcade.

Finish with a gentle garland to the right.

The Vimala Alphabet™

Uppercase

Upper zone

Baseline

Middle zone

Lower zone

Begin at the top of the upper zone, draw a straight vertical line down to the baseline.

This is called an "I am stroke"

Lift your pen or pencil off the paper, and make another "I am" stroke to the right of the first one, drawn firmly to the baseline.

Next, without lifting the pen or pencil, change direction by curving back to the left and cross over the first "I am" stroke.

Finally, form a loop behind the first "I am" stroke, and finish off to the right, beyond your second "I am" stroke.

This loop is called a "persistence tie"

Lowercase

Upper zone

Baseline

Middle zone

Lower zone

  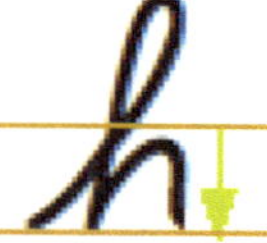 

Begin at the baseline with a soft diagonal line that gently curves to the top of the upper zone.

This is called an "ascender" or an "upstroke"

At the top of the upper zone, round leftward, curving back down to form a tall loop by crossing the first upstroke close to the baseline.

Pull to the right and away from the down-stroke.

This angle-V formation is called a "pull apart" stroke

Rounding forward at the top of the middle zone, draw back down to the base-line.

This soft arch-like formation is called an "arcade"

Finish to the right with a garland at the baseline.

The Vimala Alphabet™

The Family of Insight

- loops, retraces, and dots
- attention to detail

l

a tall loop reaching into the upper zone, just like we reach up to our greatest ideals ... and let our spirit soar.

ℓ ɛ

a small loop reaching the top of the middle zone, the teardrop *ℓ* holds our ideals in the present — tolerance and respect for others.

Epsilon *ɛ* is like two tiny c's stacked one on top of the other, both open and trusting what is in the next present moment.

ɛℓ is for "ear" ... listening from our hearts. It's a letter of kindness that complements the oval letters in the family of communication.

i

a retraced stem in the middle zone along with a well placed dot above it — clearly present and observant.

i is for "eye," the letter of clear perception and attention to details.

j

the *i* with a loop in the lower zone. *j* swallows the whole picture and turns it into a feeling sensation. Sensing situations deeply, you can feel it and taste it. Our intuitive nature.

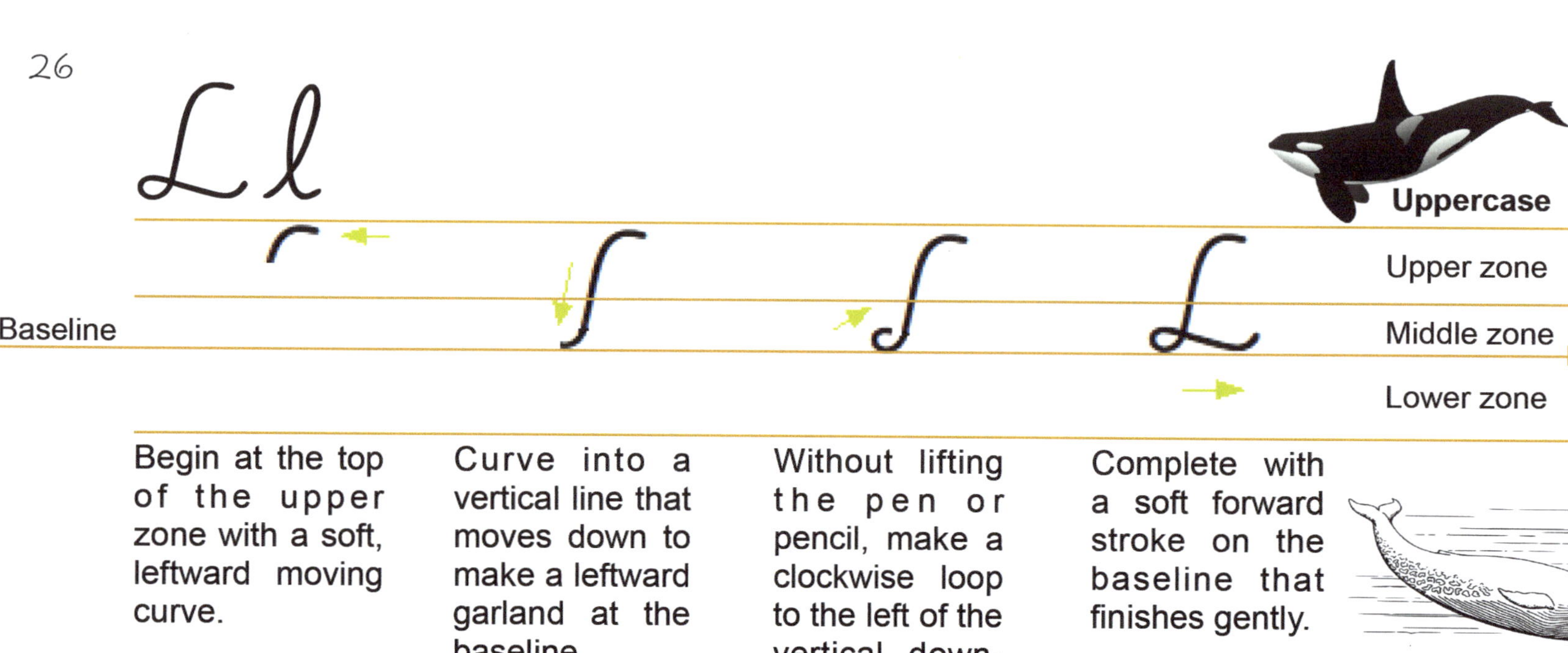

Uppercase

Upper zone

Baseline

Middle zone

Lower zone

Begin at the top of the upper zone with a soft, leftward moving curve.

Curve into a vertical line that moves down to make a leftward garland at the baseline.

Without lifting the pen or pencil, make a clockwise loop to the left of the vertical down-stroke.

Complete with a soft forward stroke on the baseline that finishes gently.

Lowercase

Upper zone

Baseline

Middle zone

Lower zone

Begin at the baseline with a soft diagonal line that gently curves to the top of the upper zone.

This is called an "ascender" or an "upstroke"

At the top of the upper zone, round leftward, curving back down to form a tall loop by crossing the first upstroke close to the baseline.

Finish with a soft garland to the right at the baseline.

The Vimala Alphabet™

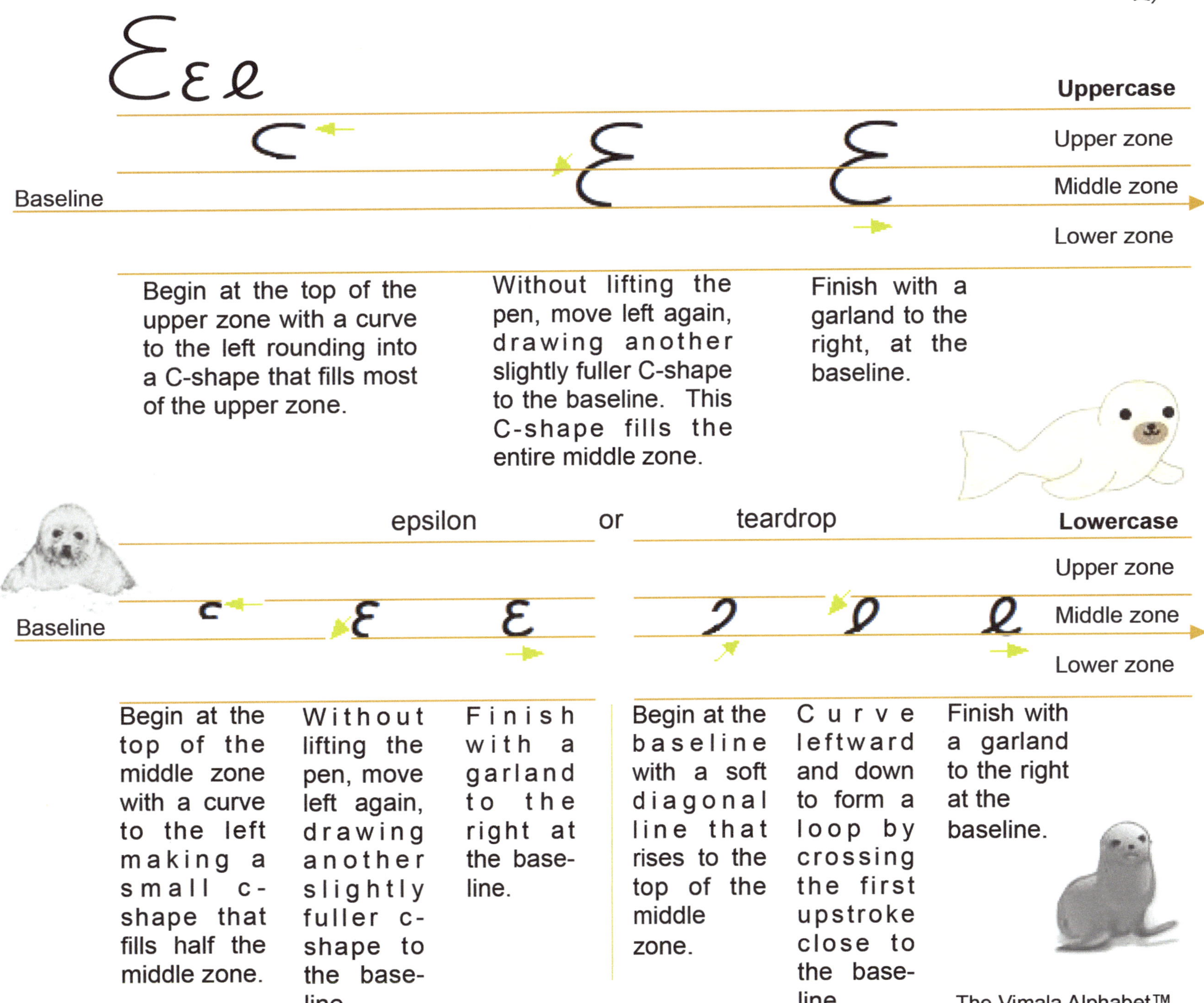

Uppercase

Upper zone

Middle zone

Baseline

Lower zone

Begin at the top of the upper zone with a curve to the left rounding into a C-shape that fills most of the upper zone.

Without lifting the pen, move left again, drawing another slightly fuller C-shape to the baseline. This C-shape fills the entire middle zone.

Finish with a garland to the right, at the baseline.

epsilon   or   teardrop

Lowercase

Upper zone

Middle zone

Baseline

Lower zone

Begin at the top of the middle zone with a curve to the left making a small c-shape that fills half the middle zone.

Without lifting the pen, move left again, drawing another slightly fuller c-shape to the baseline.

Finish with a garland to the right at the baseline.

Begin at the baseline with a soft diagonal line that rises to the top of the middle zone.

Curve leftward and down to form a loop by crossing the first upstroke close to the baseline.

Finish with a garland to the right at the baseline.

The Vimala Alphabet™

I i

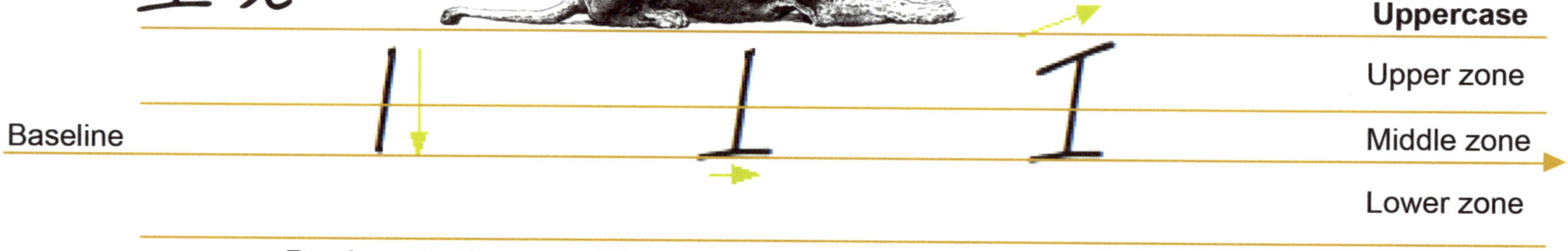

Uppercase

Upper zone

Baseline | Middle zone

Lower zone

Begin at the top of the upper zone, draw a straight vertical line down to the baseline.

This is called an "I am stroke"

Lift your pen or pencil off the paper, then draw a second line from left to right, centered horizontally across the bottom of the "I am " stroke at the baseline.

Lift your pen or pencil, off the paper again, and draw a third line from left to right, centered horizontally across the top of the "I am " stroke. Make it tilt slightly upward.

This is called a "crossbar"

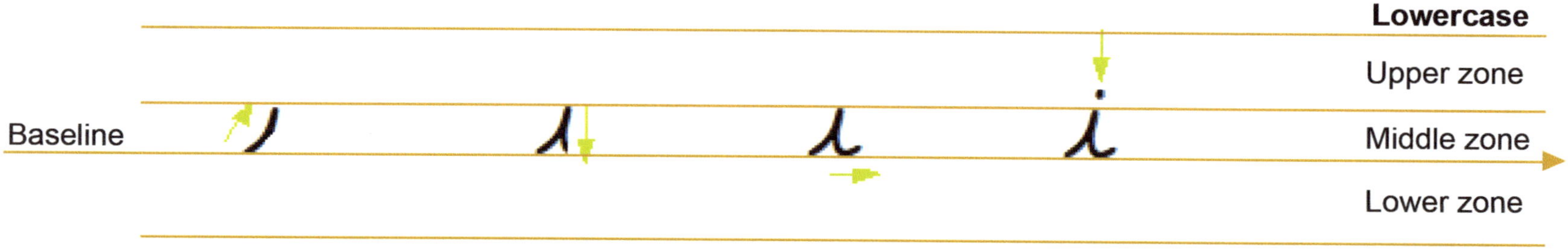

Lowercase

Upper zone

Baseline | Middle zone

Lower zone

Begin at the baseline with a soft diagonal line that gently curves to the top of the middle zone.

At the top of the middle zone, change direction by retracing back down close to the baseline.

Draw a soft garland to the right at the baseline.

Finish by placing a simple round dot just above the stem.

The Vimala Alphabet™

J j

Uppercase

Upper zone
Baseline — Middle zone
Lower zone

Begin at the baseline with a g a r l a n d moving to the left.

Continue to m o v e clockwise, to the left, and draw a g e n e r o u s half oval.

From the top of the upper z o n e, d r o p straight down to the bottom of the lower zone.

C h a n g e direction, curving to the left and up.

Finish by forming a loop up to the baseline, making a forward stroke that completes a small sideways v-formation.

Lowercase

Upper zone
Baseline — Middle zone
Lower zone

Begin at the baseline with a small garland t h a t g e n t l y curves diagonally to the top of the middle zone.

C h a n g e d i r e c t i o n, dropping to the bottom of t h e l o w e r zone.

Change direction again, rounding to the left and up with a f o r w a r d stroke past the baseline.

Finish by placing a s i m p l e round dot just above the stem.

The Family of Creativity

- balance and proportion
- "as above, so below"

f

the only lowercase letter that fills all three handwriting zones. Rising into the upper zone, *f* gives our dreams and ideas a place to live; then dips into our lower zone area of action to make those dreams come true as our gift to the world; back to the middle zone, it polishes them; and finally lets them go, unattached to how the world will receive them. It can be compared to the process of an archer's bow and arrow.

The Vimala Alphabet™

r r r

r marches along to the tune of its own drummer with all three forms fully in the middle zone.

The creative writer *r* has a little persistence tie or loop at the top of the middle zone that polishes our composition and writing skills.

The epsilon *r* resembles the epsilon ε, and brings in many talents belonging to the world of the arts.

The Tesla *r* has an angle that relishes our bringing abstract thoughts into practical use. The *r* of math and science.

r is our innate talents and true creative nature.

s

balance and grace ... a forward facing c flows downward into a backward facing c that curves gracefully into an oval bringing the flow back forward into the next present moment.

Uppercase

Upper zone

Baseline

Middle zone

Lower zone

Begin at the top of the upper zone, draw a straight vertical line down to the baseline.

This is called an "I am stroke"

Moving from left to right, draw a horizontal line touching the top of the "I am" stroke that tilts slightly upward.

Moving from left to right, draw another horizontal line halfway down, and touching the "I am" stroke.

Lowercase

Upper zone

Baseline

Middle zone

Lower zone

Begin at the baseline with a soft garland.

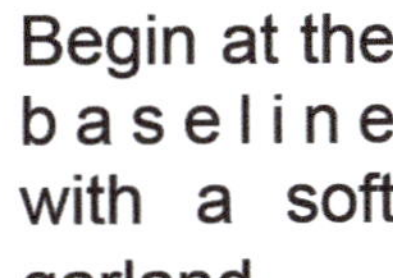

Draw up from the baseline with a soft diagonal line that curves to the top of the upper zone.

This is called an "ascender" or an "upstroke"

At the top of the upper zone, round leftward, then drop straight down to the bottom of the lower zone.

This "downstroke" is also called a "descender"

Change direction again with a soft rightward curve drawing up to form a lower loop by crossing the downstroke at the baseline.

Finally, form a little loop behind the downstroke, and finish off to the right, beyond that same downstroke, with a forward, up-stroke.

This little loop is called a "persistence tie"

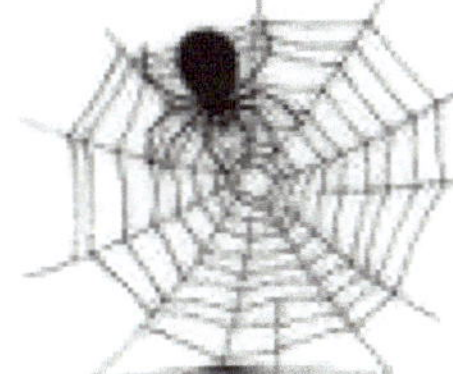

The Vimala Alphabet™

Uppercase

Upper zone

Baseline — Middle zone

Lower zone

Begin at the top of the upper zone, draw a straight vertical line down to the baseline.

This is called an "I am stroke"

Lift your pen or pencil off the paper.

Begin another horizontal line at the top of the upper zone. that curves down into a half oval that touches your "I am" stroke at the top of the middle zone.

Complete by making a rightwards diagonal line that finishes at the baseline.

Creative writer   or   Tesla r

Lowercase

Upper zone

Baseline — Middle zone

Lower zone

Begin at the baseline with a soft diagonal line that gently rises to the top of the middle zone.

At the top of the middle zone, make a small counter-clockwise loop, and move forward with a short horizontal line.

Next, draw a soft vertical line returning to the baseline, and finish with a garland to the right at the baseline.

Begin at the baseline with a soft diagonal line to the top of the middle zone.

Rounding at the top of the middle zone, draw back down to the baseline.

This soft arch-like formation is called an "arcade"

Pull to the right and away from the downstroke finishing softly at the top of the middle zone.

This angle-V formation is called a "pull apart" stroke

The Vimala Alphabet™

There are many ways to make a healthy lowercase *r.* Since it is the letter of our own innate creativity, there are as many variations in this letter as there are ways of thinking! The creative writer bubbles forth with the creative writer *r* and the Epsilon *r.* There are two other creative writing letters, the figure-8 *g* and the Epsilon ε. Writing lines of these three letters can be very useful for storytellers and composers of essays, lyrics, or articles. The next page includes the dancing *J* also because it gives so much energy and vision to our projects. There is a gentle flow in the drawing of each of these letters. Try writing a few lines of each of them. How does it feel? One word of caution, don't let your letters bow leftward from the top of the middle zone to the baseline. This is what is called a "rein-in stroke", and is to be avoided.

Rein-in strokes pull leftward from the top of the middle zone down to the baseline. These can easily happen with Epsilon *r*'s, but also occur in other letters, like *m*'s, *n*'s, and *h*'s.

Do NOT let your *r*'s pull in like this:    Avoid rein-in strokes in all letters 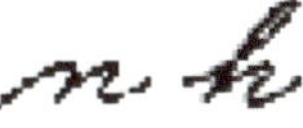

Epsilon *r*   **Lowercase**

Upper zone

Baseline   Middle zone

Lower zone

| Begin at the baseline with a soft diagonal line that gently rises to the top of the middle zone. | At the top of the middle zone, change direction by retracing a short part of the upstroke, then move right with a short horizontal stroke. | Change direction again, moving straight down to the baseline. | Finish with a soft garland to the right at the baseline. |

The Vimala Alphabet™

Creative writing letters

g   r   r   ε   т

Figure 8 g   Flat top r   Epsilon r   Epsilon e   Dancing t

Practice words

great   target   egret   gargle   Trigonometry   progress   register

The Vimala Alphabet™

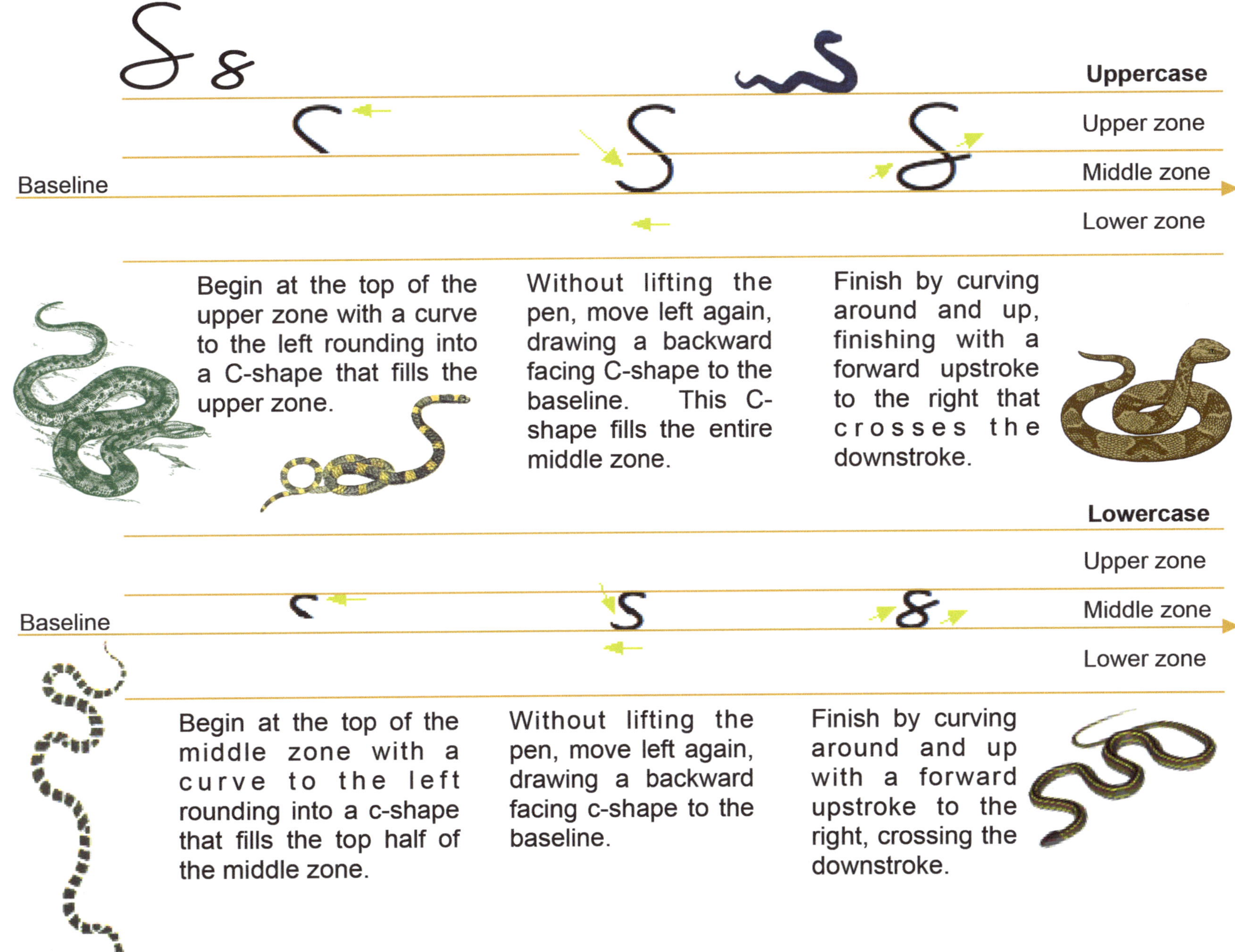

Uppercase

Upper zone

Baseline

Middle zone

Lower zone

Begin at the top of the upper zone with a curve to the left rounding into a C-shape that fills the upper zone.

Without lifting the pen, move left again, drawing a backward facing C-shape to the baseline. This C-shape fills the entire middle zone.

Finish by curving around and up, finishing with a forward upstroke to the right that crosses the downstroke.

Lowercase

Upper zone

Baseline

Middle zone

Lower zone

Begin at the top of the middle zone with a curve to the left rounding into a c-shape that fills the top half of the middle zone.

Without lifting the pen, move left again, drawing a backward facing c-shape to the baseline.

Finish by curving around and up with a forward upstroke to the right, crossing the downstroke.

The Family of Status

- vision, decision, forward thinking strokes
- "I am" strokes show great determination
- crossbar
- sideways v

retraced upstroke shows how tall we stand in the world; the crossbar at the top puts our goals high and speaks of a far reaching vision.

The crossbar is the singular stroke in handwriting showing our will power, particularly in the work area. It needs to be firmly drawn.

The "dancing-ℑ" brings in an element of fun as well as determination. It says action!

There are NO loops in ℐ-stems:  Stems are simply retraced:

an "I am" stroke with a sideways v touching the right side. It says,

"I am discerning"
and
"I choose for myself"

an "I am" stroke with a half oval that flows around and forward into the present ... aligning self with the business of "I am" making a living. Bringing personal values into the work arena.

Uppercase

Upper zone

Baseline — Middle zone

Lower zone

Begin at the top of the upper zone, draw a straight vertical line down to the baseline.

This is called an "I am stroke"

Lift your pen or pencil off the paper, and draw a second line from left to right, centered horizontally across the top of the "I am " stroke. Make it tilt slightly upward.

This is called the "crossbar"

Lowercase

Basic t   or   Dancing t

Upper zone

Baseline — Middle zone

Lower zone

Begin softly at the baseline drawing a line up to the top of the upper zone.

This is called an "ascender" or an "upstroke"

Changing direction, retrace back down to the baseline, drawing a garland to the right.

Lift your pen or pencil off the paper. Draw a centered horizontal line at the top of the t-stem.

Begin at the baseline with a garland, and curve up to the top of the upper zone.

An introductory garland is called "Lincoln foot".

Next, change direction, and draw a straight vertical line down to the baseline.

This is called an "I am stroke"

Now change direction again by curving back to the left. Crossing over the first "upstroke" line you made …

Finally, form a loop at the top of the t-stem, behind the upstroke, and finish off to the right, forming the crossbar.

This little loop is called a "persistence tie"

The Vimala Alphabet™

K k

Uppercase

Upper zone

Baseline — Middle zone

Lower zone

Begin at the top of the upper zone, draw a straight vertical line down to the baseline.

This is called an "I am stroke"

Lift your pen or pencil off the paper.

Begin another diagonal line leftward from the top of the upper zone to the top of the middle zone, so that it touches your "I am" stroke.

Complete the sideways angle-v by making a rightwards diagonal line that finishes at the baseline.

Lowercase

Upper zone

Baseline — Middle zone

Lower zone

Begin at the top of the upper zone, draw a straight vertical line down to the baseline.

This is called an "I am stroke"

Lift your pen or pencil off the paper.

Begin another diagonal line leftward from the top of the middle zone to the middle of the middle zone, so that it touches your "I am" stroke.

Complete the sideways angle-v by making a rightwards diagonal line that finishes at the baseline.

The Vimala Alphabet™

B b

Uppercase

Upper zone

Baseline — Middle zone

Lower zone

I T P B B

Begin at the top of the upper zone, draw a straight vertical line down to the baseline.	Lift your pen or pencil off the paper.	Round down to just above the top of the middle zone, making a half circle.	Make a second rightward, downward curve, forming another slightly fuller half circle that touches your "I am" stroke at the baseline.	Complete by turning and curving to the right as you loop through your half oval and finish to the right of your "I am stroke".
This is called an "I am stroke"				

Lowercase

Upper zone

Baseline — Middle zone

Lower zone

I t b b

Begin at the top of the upper zone, draw a straight vertical line down to the baseline.	Lift your pen or pencil off the paper.	Make it round down to the baseline so it forms a half circle when it touches your "I am stroke".	Complete by turning and curving to the right as you loop through your half oval and finish to the right of your "I am stroke."
This is called an "I am stroke"	Begin a soft horizontal line at the top of the middle zone.		

The Vimala Alphabet™

The Family of Trust and Inner Authority

- curves and angles ...
- both are a portrayal of openness
- being present with a readiness to meet the future

C

a soft, clear arc ... open to the future, trusting. The circle or oval self without closure; looking forward to what's ahead.   Trusting from out heart center.

X

four v's around a center, our inner self, our inner authority.   Seeing all sides of an issue, and approaching life with integrity;   being centered.   Acting on principles of what we know to be true.

C c

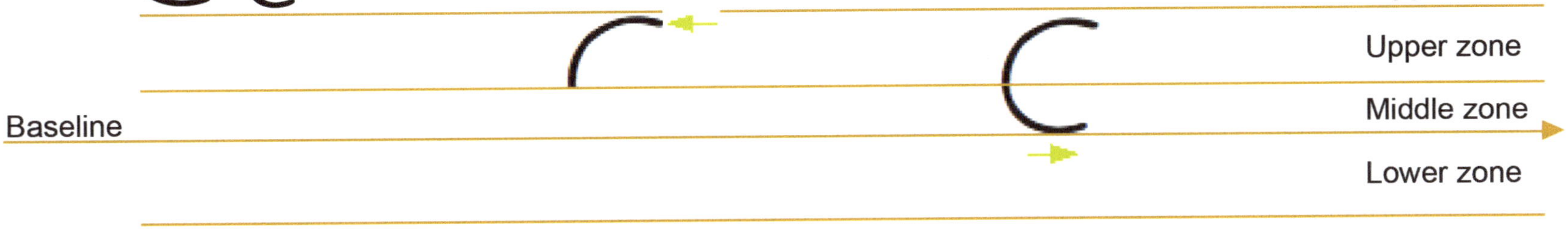

Uppercase

Upper zone

Baseline — Middle zone

Lower zone

Begin at the top of the upper zone with a soft curve to the left.

Continue curving around to form a half circle that fills both the upper and middle zones, and finish softly at the baseline.

Lowercase

Upper zone

Baseline — Middle zone

Lower zone

Begin at the top of the middle zone with a soft curve to the left.

Continue curving around to form a half circle that fills the whole middle zone, and finish softly at the baseline.

The Vimala Alphabet™

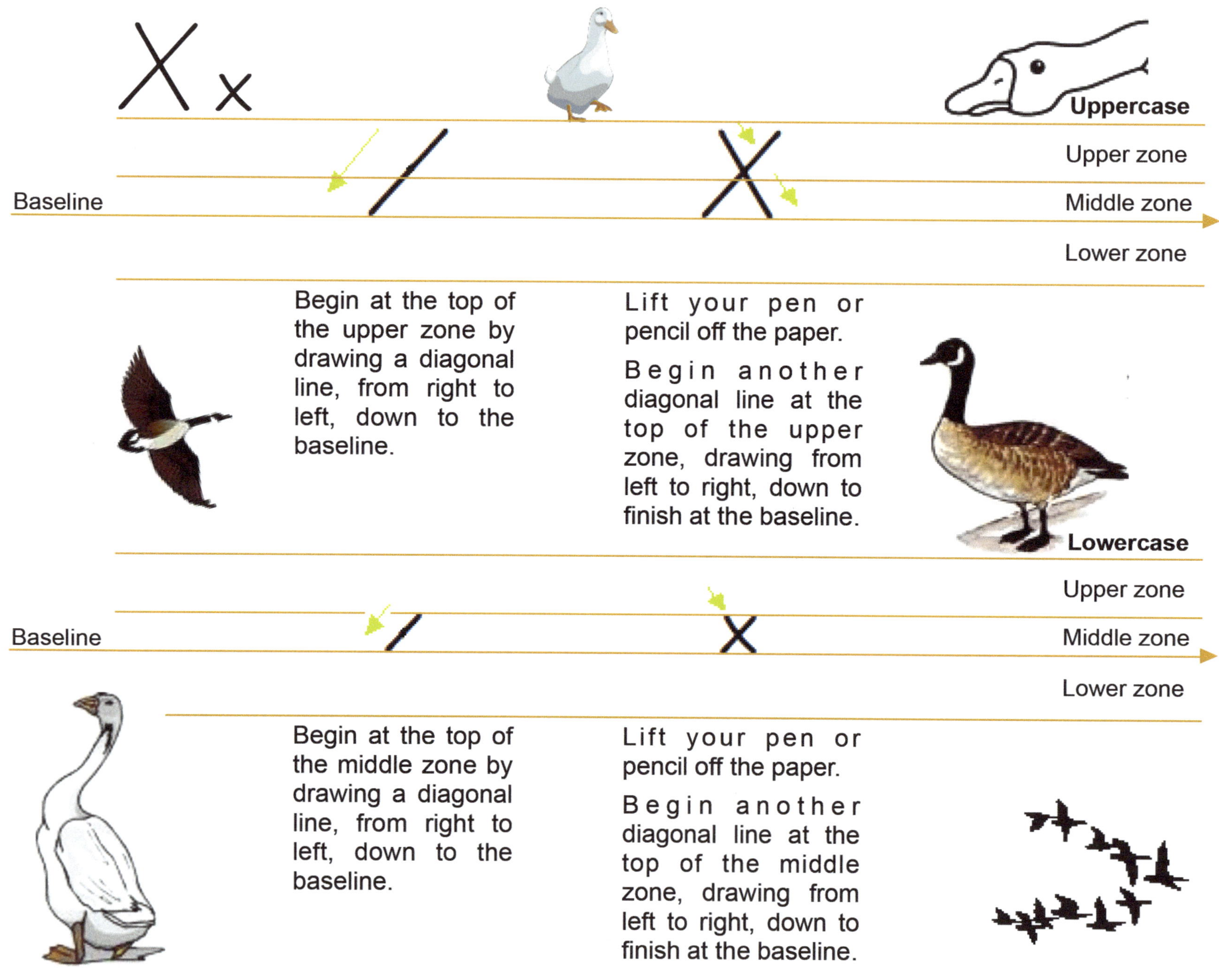

Begin at the top of the upper zone by drawing a diagonal line, from right to left, down to the baseline.

Lift your pen or pencil off the paper.

Begin another diagonal line at the top of the upper zone, drawing from left to right, down to finish at the baseline.

Begin at the top of the middle zone by drawing a diagonal line, from right to left, down to the baseline.

Lift your pen or pencil off the paper.

Begin another diagonal line at the top of the middle zone, drawing from left to right, down to finish at the baseline.

The Vimala Alphabet™

Grandfather Zed

- balance
- uncharged stability
- letter of contentment and a happy heart

Looking back on past experiences, the Grandfather Zed stands content. Taking in all the qualities from his extended family of letters ... Ʒ is happy and at peace ... life is good.

Uppercase

Upper zone

Baseline

Middle zone

Lower zone

Beginning at the top of the upper zone, round to the right and draw a soft half circle down to the top of the middle zone.

From the top of the middle zone, curve down to the bottom of the lower zone.

Round to the left at the bottom of the lower zone, and begin to loop up.

Finish the loop up to the baseline and finish off to the right of the first downstroke.

Lowercase

Upper zone

Baseline

Middle zone

Lower zone

Beginning at the top of the middle zone, round rightward and draw a soft half circle down to the baseline.

From the baseline, draw down to the bottom of the lower zone.

Round to the left at the bottom of the lower zone, and begin to loop up.

Finish the loop up to the baseline and finish off to the right of the first downstroke.

The Vimala Alphabet™

The Ampersand: shorthand for "and"; "et" is the Latin word for "and".

The Ampersand is a little ligature that has survived from ancient times when scribes created it as a brief symbol to copy "additionally", "in addition" or the word "and" into their manuscripts.

Upper zone

Baseline — Middle zone — Lower zone

Begin at the top of the middle zone by making a leftward curve that forms the upper c-shape of an epsilon e.

Curve down to the baseline making another larger C-shape, completing the epsilon ε.

Draw a soft garland half way up the height of the middle zone; change direction, and draw a vertical line straight down to the baseline.

At the baseline, change direction again moving left and diagonally back to the top of the middle zone

Finish to the right with a soft T-crossbar that tilts upward.

Practice Sentence:

Handwriting is letters & words & sentences & paragraphs.

Joining the letters — the art of cursive writing

Connectivity

Now that we've walked through the Alphabet, it's time to put our letters together.

Garland endings flow naturally to garland beginnings.   Bridge strokes reach from one letter to the next.

Let breaks occur every three to five letters.   Breaks occur naturally when we lift our pen to dot an i or cross a t.

Tried   Tonal   little   pasteurized

Breaks are efficient when one letter stops at the baseline and another begins at the top of the middle or upper zone.

look   started   flyer   darted   drinking   king

Breaks are efficient when one letter stops at the top of the middle or upper zone and another begins at the baseline.

red   charter   vertical   ripe   friction

Breaks always occur before and after the letters *v, k, x,* and the stand alone *o.*

baker   boxer   braver

In the next section we will learn about ligatures.   Ligatures are formed when the finishing part of one letter flows into the beginning stroke of the next letter.   Ligatures always stand alone in a word, so breaks occur naturally before and after a ligature.

The Vimala Alphabet™

Garlands	*a d u m n h l e e i r t c*
join	*and lunch*
Bridge strokes	*w o*
join	*we our*
Up strokes	*y g j z*
join or do not join	*year good jeep zip*
Forward strokes	*q f p s b*
join or do not join	*quiet feel pen sun best*
Angle strokes	*v k x*
do not join	*even owl keep box*

The Th th Ligature

The term 'ligature' comes from the Latin word *ligat* or *ligatura* meaning 'bound.' The reference is to anything that's used to tie or fasten two things together. It can also be used as a verb, coming from the Latin *ligare*, to bind.

Musically, the word relates to the Latin *legato*, meaning to play a group of two or more notes together as one harmonious sound. In handwriting, a ligature consists of two or more letters that join in such a way that they create a new combination letter. Ligatures, like the letters k, x and v, stand alone in a word. They do not join any other letters, whether at their beginning or finish.

––––––––––––––

There are two other variations called the 'Dancing Th' Ligature. These are made in one continuous movement, without lifting the pen: Th Th

The simpler version illustrated here, th, is easier for children to master.

	thick
	thin
Beginning of a word:	thought
	thanks
	lather
In the middle of a word:	feather
	wither
	withheld
	faith
Ending a word:	bath
	math
	hearth

The Vimala Alphabet™

Th th

Uppercase

Upper zone

Baseline — Middle zone

Lower zone

Begin at the top of the upper zone, draw a straight vertical line down to the baseline.

This is called an "I am stroke"

Lift your pen or pencil off the paper.

Begin another horizontal line, slightly bowed, at the top of the upper zone.

This is called an "umbrella stroke"

From the top of the upper zone, drop straight down to the baseline.

Pull up and to the right, away from the downstroke; and draw an arcade.

This angle-V formation is called a "pull apart" stroke

Finish with a soft garland to the right at the baseline.

Lowercase

Upper zone

Baseline — Middle zone

Lower zone

Begin softly at the baseline drawing a line up to the top of the upper zone.

This is called an "ascender" or an "upstroke"

Changing direction, retrace back down to the baseline, making a garland to the right.

Lift your pen or pencil off the paper.

Draw a centered horizontal line at the top of the t-stem.

Round up and left, making a counter-clockwise loop, then draw down to the baseline.

Pull up and to the right, away from the downstroke; and draw an arcade.

This angle-V formation is called a "pull apart" stroke

Finish with a soft garland, ending to the right at the baseline.

The Vimala Alphabet™

Rule-of-Thumb Pointers

Quick reference guides to apply throughout your handwriting

The goal of writing is to have clear, clean letters. Write simply and clearly. This does not mean perfection! Writing is meant to be fun, with a casual, balanced overall appearance. After all, it needs to be fun for the person who will read our writing too.

Balanced overall appearance means that the lower loops of letters need to be just as long as the upper loops so there is a nice balance in the overall appearance. A good rule-of-thumb is that the upper and lower zones are about two to two-and-a-half times as tall and long as the middle zone. Loops are like containers. They give our ideas and dreams a place to live. Make sure they have lots of room to breathe!

Most letters and all numerals are made from beginning to finish without lifting the pen or pencil. The exceptions being the letters *Đ, G, Q, Pp, H, Ii, j, F, R, TI, Kk, Bb,* and *Xx.*

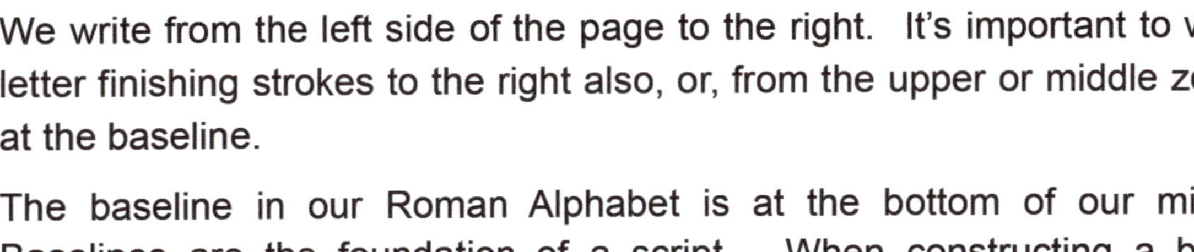

We write from the left side of the page to the right. It's important to write all our letter finishing strokes to the right also, or, from the upper or middle zones, finish at the baseline.

The baseline in our Roman Alphabet is at the bottom of our middle zone. Baselines are the foundation of a script. When constructing a building, it's important to build a good foundation. In writing it's just as important to keep our baselines level.

Do NOT retrace down strokes! *Mm, Nn, h.* These are called "pull-apart" strokes; they form little v's as they pull away from the down stroke.

Do retrace up strokes! *d T* There should be no loops in these d and t stems.

Space is important in life and in handwriting! Crowded letters and words look cramped and uncomfortable. Give your handwriting room to breathe.

The goal is to write on unlined paper. A blank page allows for our own individual expression of life. There is little creativity or free thinking when confined to the boundaries of lines. Give your hand the freedom to create its own sense of space.

The Vimala Alphabet™

To practice your Vimala Alphabet letters with pen or pencil, you can photocopy the following pages. Use a thin piece of paper to lay over the lines or the letters for tracing. These can serve as gentle guides until you are more familiar with the letters. The first set is for beginners, and has larger letters and wider line spacing. When you feel comfortable, discard these sheets, and let your writing flow onto a blank page of unlined paper. Remember to write in the landscape direction, lengthwise across the page. If you find your baselines are climbing uphill or slipping downhill, simply fold your paper in half, then unfold it, and use the fold line as a gentle reminder to keep your beautiful letters heading level across the page.

As you become a skilled writer you will want to create your own autograph. Practice your autograph! Make your signature shine. Underscore it! Sticker it with your Alphabet animal.

Master your letters! Choose two or three letters to practice. For each letter, write three lines of the lowercase and uppercase. Next write a line of words that begin with that letter, another line of words that end in that letter, and finally, a line of words with that letter in the middle of the word. You can be creative and find words that contain two or three of the letters you want to practice, condensing your word lines to include both or all three letters. For example:

w, f, l: wolf flow lawful　　or　　*a, c, r: arc car racer area*

Write in the landscape direction

The Vimala Alphabet™

The Vimala Alphabet™
Practice Pages

Background Guidelines for beginning writers
Cursive Letters for Tracing

These pages are intended for beginning students' practice,
and should be discarded as they become familiar with the letters

Background baselines for the youngest writers - use only as needed behind blank pages as a gentle reminder for beginners *a a a o o o o o o d d d*

g g g g g p p p y y y

u u u w w w w v v v

m m m n n n h h h

l l l ε ε ε e e i i i j j j

Background letters for tracing for the youngest writers - use only as needed behind blank pages as a gentle reminder for beginners

The Vimala Alphabet™

Background letters for tracing for the youngest writers - use only as needed behind blank pages as a gentle reminder for beginners

A O D G Q P

Y U W V M N

H L E I J

F R S T K B

C X Z Th &

Background letters for tracing for the youngest writers - use only as needed behind blank pages as a gentle reminder for beginners

Background baselines for young writers - use only as needed behind blank pages as a gentle reminder

a a a a a a a   A A A A

o o o o o o o   O O O O

d d d d d d d   Đ Đ Đ Đ

8 8 8 8 8 8 8   G G G G

q q q q q q q   Q Q Q Q

p p p p p p p   P P P P

Background letters for tracing for young writers - use only as needed behind blank pages as a gentle reminder

The Vimala Alphabet™

h h h h h h
l l l l l l l l
e e e e ε ε ε ε
i i i i i i i i
j j j j j j j
f f f f f f f f

H H H
L L L
Ɛ Ɛ Ɛ
I I I
ʃ ʃ ʃ
F F F

Background letters for tracing for young writers - use only as needed behind blank pages as a gentle reminder

The Vimala Alphabet™

ɲ ɲ ɲ ɲ   N N N   R R R

8 8 8 8 8 8 8 8   S S S

TT TT TT TT ᛏ ᛏ ᛏ   T T T

k k k k k k k k k   K K K

b b b b b b b b b   B B B

c c c c c c c c c   C C C

Background letters for tracing for young writers - use only as needed behind blank pages as a gentle reminder

x x x x x x x x x   X X X

з з з з з з з з з   з з з

th th th th th   Th Th Th

ઠ ઠ ઠ ઠ ઠ ઠ ઠ

1 2 3 4 5 6 7 8 9 0

Background letters for tracing for young writers - use only as needed behind blank pages as a gentle reminder

Outline letters for the very young

Outline letters for the very young

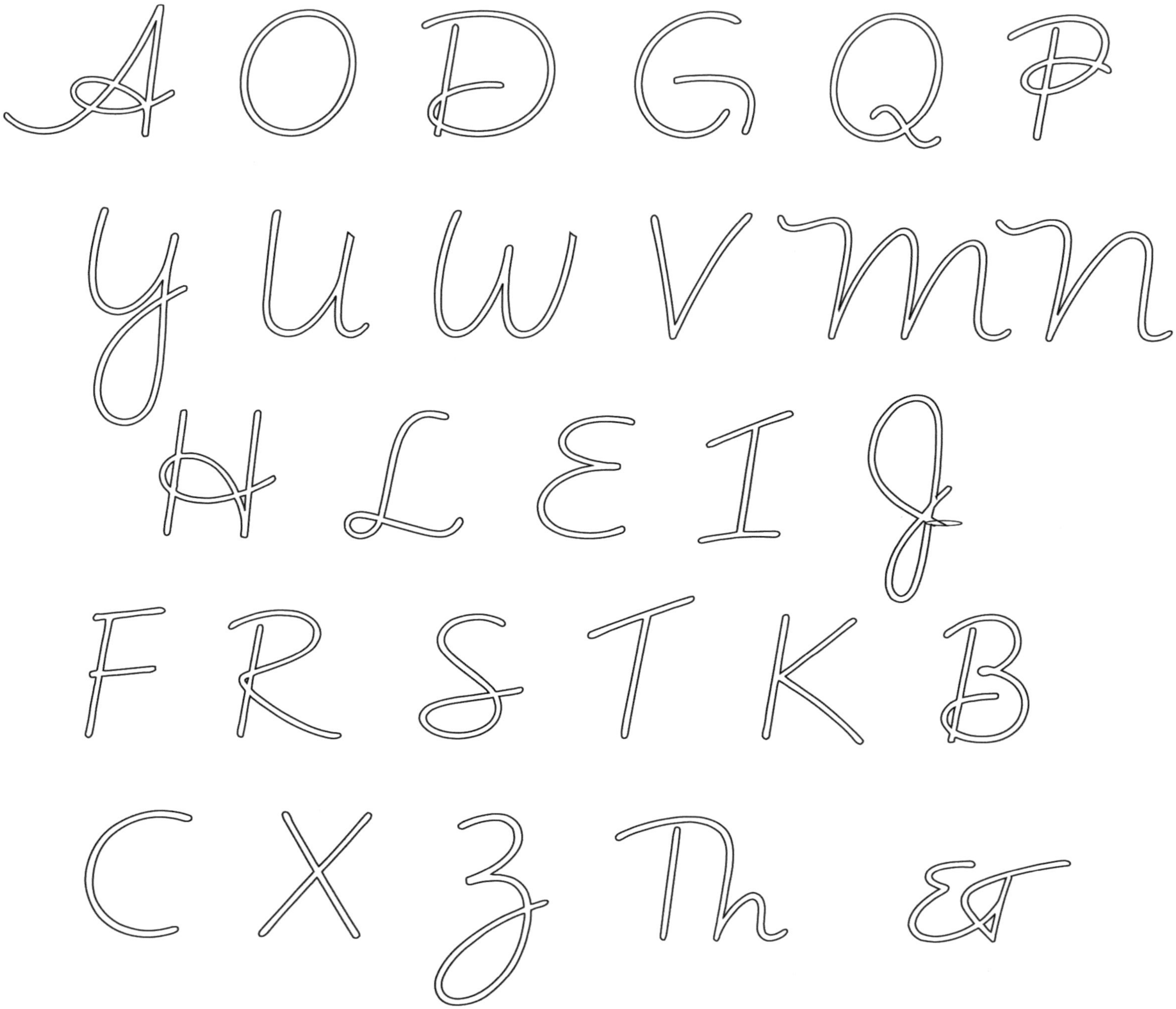

Outline letters for the very young

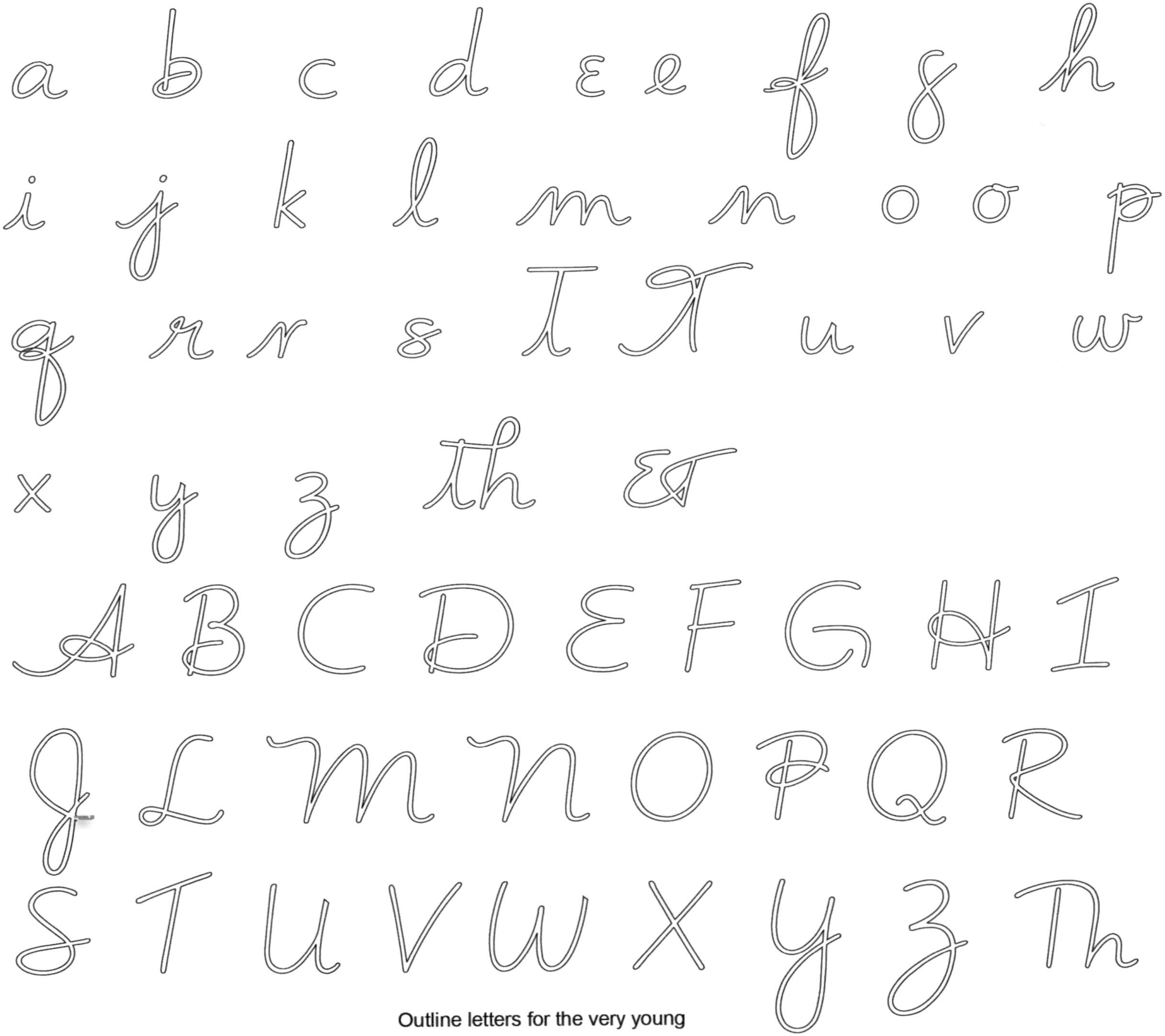

a b c d e f g h
i j k l m n o p
q r s t u v w
x y z th &

A B C D E F G H I
J L M N O P Q R
S T U V W X Y Z Th

Outline letters for the very young

Glossary

ampersand - an abbreviated symbol for the word "and"   & *&* See page 45

angle - V-formations pointed at the baseline *Vv*

arcade - an archway shape. *M m N n h* See page 21

ascender - a handwriting stroke that rises up from the baseline into the upper zone.

baseline - the imaginary line our handwritten letters sit or run upon, the foundation for our letters.
     See page 6

bridge stroke - a short horizontal rightward stroke at the top of the middle zone.   At the end of
certain letters it is used to connect to the next letter. *w o* This stroke enhances manual dexterity.

capital - an uppercase letter. Also see uppercase.

connecting strokes - see page 46
     garland - a soft cup like stroke at the baseline
     arcade - an arch shaped stroke
     angle - a v-like shaped stroke at the baseline
     wedge - an inverted v-stroke at the baseline
     thread - a squiggly worm like stroke close to the baseline
     bridge stroke - a short horizontal line at the top of the middle zone, *w o*
     upstroke - a line that ascends from the baseline or from the lower zone.
     forward stroke - a line that moves horizontally, or almost horizontally to the right

crossbar - the horizontal stroke that crosses the *T*-stem and uppercase *I*. See pages 37 and 28

cursive - writing that joins the letters within words; literally cursive means "running."

descender - a handwriting stroke that dips into the lower zone.

dominant hand - the hand we use to write with.

downstroke - a handwriting stroke that moves downward; also a descender. See also descender.

epsilon - the fifth letter of the Greek Alphabet, transliterated 'e'. Term for our Roman 'e' that resembles it.

flourish - an added stroke to a letter or letters, usually artfully creative, or can be very elaborate. Also see humor flourish.

font - the term for a style of computer generated letter forms. Examples: Ariel, Schoolhouse, Mona Lisa, Monaco, Papyrus, Courier, Comic Sans MS.

garland - a soft cup-like handwriting stroke, often occurring between letters within words or at the end of letters.

handwriting - the art or act of writing letters with a pen or pencil by hand. A handwritten sample of letters or words. Also see cursive.

humor flourish - a soft, casual introductory stroke at the top of the upper zone: *m n*

"I am" stroke - a straight, vertical firmly drawn line from the top of the upper zone to the baseline.

landscape layout / direction - paper laid out for writing across the longest or widest side. Also see portrait. See page 50

letter - a grapheme. A symbol for a language sound, or phoneme.

ligature - a combination letter where an ending portion of one letter joins the next letter by forming its beginning stroke. See page 47.

Lincoln foot - an introductory garland named for President Abraham Lincoln because he introduced his autograph with it. *A* and the dancing *A* and dancing *Th Th* ligature.

loops - an elongated shape made by a curve that bends around and crosses itself near the baseline. There are upper loops and lower loops. In handwriting, all loops are containers for things ... ideas, imagination, dreams, thoughts, creativity.

lowercase - the small letters used in common words and within sentences.

margins - the spaces around a page of writing. There is a top and bottom margin; and a left (where our writing begins on every line of a page) and a right margin (where our writing ends on most lines of a page). The right margin is the only one that may have a ragged edge on a page because words end randomly.

midzone - another way of saying "the middle zone". Also see zones. See pages 6 and 7.

non-dominant hand - the hand we do NOT write with.

numeral - a symbol that represents a number. Included in the practice pages.

persistence tie - a tie loop that goes behind a letter, loops, then flies forward. *f q T A H*
It says, "I can do anything I set my mind to do, nothing can stop me!"

portrait layout / direction - paper laid out for writing across the shortest or narrowest side. Also see landscape layout / direction.   See page 50

print - a form of writing that does not join the letters, usually made using straight and curved lines.   / + \ + - = A   or   (+) = 0

printscript - a term for a simplified handwriting that incorporates both cursive and printed letters, usually simplified uppercase letters such as the Vimala *O, G, Q, P, U, W, V, M, n, H, I, F, R, S, T, K, B, C, X,* etc.

pull-apart stroke - in the midzone, this stroke pulls away from the downstroke of an arcade rather than retracing it.   It makes a little v-formation at the baseline. *M m, N n, h* It's a rule-of-thumb NOT to retrace downstrokes! See pages 49.

rein-in - an equestrian term for slowing a horse, pulling back on the reins. Rein in strokes in handwriting are most frequently found in arcades, letters *m n h,* and also in epsilon *r*'s.

Avoid making these: *m n h r*
As the pen draws the letter, it pulls back, curling leftward on the right side of the arcade or letter. It's like kicking a horse to run, but reining him in at the same time. The curling in on the finishing side enforces an unhealthy restraint of all our efforts   See page 33.

rule-of-thumb - a generally accepted way of doing something.

slant - the direction the handwritten letters tend to tilt: left (backward), right (forward), or not leaning in either direction, but standing vertical.

spacing - a term used for margins, and also for the allowance given to letters within words and between words, whether crowed, cramped, stretched, or casually flowing.

tangled lines - handwriting that writes through the lower loops descending from the line above. Also upper loops that invade into the line above. It's a rule-of-thumb to give ample spacing to handwritten lines.

tie stroke - see "persistence tie" *f g A H T Th*

umbrella stroke - a convex curved crossbar that enhances self-discipline. *Th*

uppercase - a capital letter used at the beginning of a sentence and for all proper names. Also see capital.

upstroke - a handwriting stroke that moves upward; also an ascender. Also see ascender.

Vimala Alphabet - A writing system created by Vimala Rodgers that incorporates all the best aspects of the Roman letters.

wedge - an inverted v-formation found within letters or letter connections within words.

zones - The three sections in a line of handwriting:
upper zone: above the middle zone
middle zone (midzone): baseline to bottom of upper zone
lower zone: below the baseline   See pages 6 and 7

A	Dolphin	*L*	Whale
O	Hawk	*E*	Baby Harp Seal
D	Dog	*I*	Lioness
G	Elk	*J*	Bear
Q	Horse		
P	Porcupine	*F*	Spider
		R	Silkworm
Y	Peahen	*S*	Snake
U	Owl		
W	Wolf	*T*	Tiger
V	Eagle	*K*	Deer
		B	Camel
M	Swan		
N	Chimpanzee	*C*	White Buffalo
H	Butterfly	*X*	Goose

Z Pelican

Th Hummingbird